PICTURES IN *n* EEDLEWORK

PICTURES IN nEEDLEWORK

SHELLEY FAYE LAZAR

Macmillan Publishing Company
New York

Maxwell Macmillan International
New York   Oxford   Singapore   Sydney

Macmillan Publishing Company
866 Third Avenue, New York, NY 10022

Collier Macmillan Canada, Inc.
1200 Eglinton Avenue East, Suite 200
Don Mills, Ontario M3C 3N1

Library of Congress Cataloging-in-Publication Data

Lazar, Shelley Faye.
    Pictures in needlework/Shelley Faye Lazar.
        p.   cm.
    ISBN 0-02-569510-X
    1. Embroidery—Patterns.   2. Tapestry.   3. Fabric pictures.
I. Title.
TT771.L33   1990
746.3—dc20   90-6115
                                                                                CIP

Macmillan books are available at special discounts for bulk purchases for sales
promotions, premiums, fund-raising, or educational use. For details, contact:

Special Sales Director
Macmillan Publishing Company
866 Third Avenue
New York, NY 10022

Designed by Janet James
Photography by Michele Rogers
Stitch diagrams by Kate Simunek
Technical Editor: Judith Casey

10   9   8   7   6   5   4   3   2   1

Printed in Great Britain

A selection of Shelley Faye Lazar kits are available
and are distributed in the U.S.A. by Plymouth Yarn Co.,
P.O. Box 28, 500 Lafayette Street, Bristol, PA 19007.

IMPORTANT NOTE

The measurements in this book are given in both inches and centimetres.
Please note that the first measurement given is always the height and the
second measurement is the width.

CONTENTS

FOREWORD

Within this book are many ideas for stitching original pictures to celebrate special occasions. Each picture makes a perfect gift, eventually becoming a treasured keepsake.

A traditional stitched sampler was originally a test-piece for practising different stitches, and the worker personalized it by including a name and date. In this way samplers became keepsakes and time pieces. My 'samplers' are designed for specific occasions but they also give great scope for you to adapt them and make them more individual.

The stitched design of each picture expresses the main theme of the gift. The illustrations on the mount (mat board) extend the message, complementing the embroidery with similar colours but obviously giving a contrasting texture.

One of my aims when creating the designs was that you should enjoy exploring the range of possibilities within a variety of simple stitches. The threads provide a kaleidoscope of colours and textures to give inspiration. The simple designs allow you to experiment and create wonderful visual effects, such as mixing your own coloured thread. Beads and sequins add sparkle and an extra dimension.

The main reason for sewing and decorating the pictures is enjoyment; in the making, and the giving and the receiving. With this in mind, the designs are kept simple so that even a beginner can complete the designs very easily and quickly. There is no need to master any complicated techniques and all the materials should be available from good craft shops.

I hope these designs inspire you to sew the pictures and go on to develop your own ideas and techniques.

Shelley Faye Lazar

INTRODUCTION

Canvas

The needlepoint pictures in this book all use single-thread canvas of either 22, 18 or 10 threads to 1in (2.5cm). The two small meshes (22 and 18) enable you to produce very fine work. When buying canvas always allow a margin of about 2–3in (5–8cm) around the area to be stitched. This leaves room for mounting on stretcher frames or handling while stitching, and final stretching and mounting when completed.

Embroidery fabric

You can use almost any smooth, closely woven fabric for surface embroidery, but heavy-weight calico (unbleached muslin) has been specified for the designs in this book, because it is economical and versatile and will take a variety of heavy and light-weight threads without distorting or puckering unduly. It has a plain (common) weave, allowing even and easy stitching. Its neutral colour is ideal for painting in different colours; left plain, it gives a good foundation for colourful embroidery threads. However, a medium-weight calico (muslin) could be used instead, or a medium- or heavy-weight linen.

Thread

Your choice of thread is almost unlimited bearing in mind a couple of points. The thread should not be so thick that it pulls and distorts the canvas making it uncomfortable to stitch. Conversely it should not be too thin to cover the material. When stitching, do not make the length of thread in the needle too long otherwise it will twist into knots or wear thin before it is finished.

In general, the threads for the needlepoint pictures in this book are specified. The main types of thread are 6-stranded cotton (embroidery floss) and 3-stranded wool. All these threads are widely available in a range of colours. You can develop your skills further by experimenting with other threads such as *coton perlé* (available in various thicknesses), tapestry and knitting yarns, *coton à broder* (also called brilliant embroidery cotton – very thin), soft cotton (retours) and even raffia or string.

In all the projects, the successful and effective combination of fabric, thread and stitch is based on their suitability for the design and their relation to each other.

Needles

For needlepoint, use a tapestry needle which has a rounded point. Tapestry needles are available in a range of sizes. The size selected is governed by the mesh of canvas, so that the needle passes through easily without distorting the canvas. For example, you use a size 22 needle for 22 mesh canvas. The thread chosen must pass easily through the eye of the needle without fraying while stitching.

For embroidery on a closely woven fabric, the same rules apply, but the needle must have a sharp point. You can use crewel or chenille needles, though generally crewel needles are for finer fabrics.

Stretcher frames

Canvas Ideally, mount the canvas on a frame, so that the canvas is evenly stretched. Artists' stretcher frames are available in pairs to any length, and therefore can make up to any square or rectangular shape. Staple, pin or tack the canvas centrally to the frame.
Embroidery fabric An embroidery frame keeps your work flat and even when sewing closely worked stitches. Embroidery hoops, available in various sizes, consist of two rings closely fitting inside each other to hold the fabric taut. Alternatively use artists' stretcher frames, as with the canvas.

Because all the embroidery projects in this book are small, you may find it unnecessary to use a frame, and decide to simply hold the canvas in your hand. One should also take care to watch that the material does not distort or pucker.

Stitching

There are 15 different stitches in this book. For step-by-step instructions, please refer to pages 93–96.

At the start of stitching, push the needle and thread through the material on the front/right side, a little distance from the area you are about to work. When your stitches cover the thread, trim off the loose end. To finish off the length of thread, darn it through previously made stitches on the reverse/wrong side of your work.

It is not advisable to make embroidery or needlepoint stitches in just one movement, especially if the fabric is stretched on a frame. For the purposes of illustration, diagrams usually show a stitch being made all in one movement. To make the stitches correctly, use the 'two hand' method. Insert the needle down through the canvas with the hand on top of the frame, and with the hand below the frame pull the needle through. Push the needle back up with the hand under the frame and follow by pulling through with the hand on top. With practice and speed, you can achieve a regular stitch. Keep the tension even by not pulling the thread too tightly.

Avoid using knots to secure the thread when starting or finishing off, because they can cause bumps in the finished article, when mounted.

Using charts

Canvas The majority of needlepoint pictures in this book are shown on graph charts. Coloured lines indicate the colour of thread and also the length and direction (vertical or horizontal) of stitch. Each line on the graph represents a canvas thread. Therefore, if a red coloured line extends over four lines vertically, this means you work a vertical straight stitch in red over the four canvas threads.

Tent stitch is represented on the charts by small diagonal lines intersecting the canvas threads. Beads and French knots, are indicated by small circles on the charts.

If in any doubt, you can cross refer from the charts to the photographs of the pictures, shown life size. Always remember there is no such thing as a mistake. Your picture can vary from the designs here by change of colour or size, to put your personal stamp on it.

In some instances, instead of a chart you can transfer the designs directly on to the canvas by tracing with dressmaker's carbon paper or drawing free hand with a soft pencil or a pale-coloured felt tip. If you want to enlarge or reduce the design, take a coarser or finer mesh canvas and transfer the design square by square on to your canvas.

Embroidery fabric To transfer the designs on to fabric, first make a tracing from the black and white illustration shown in the project. Lay this centrally on top of your fabric with a sheet of dressmakers' carbon paper in between. Draw over the lines so that an impression is made on the fabric. All the lines will eventually be concealed with stitches.

An alternative method is to tape the tracing of the design to a window with light or sun shining through. Tape your fabric centrally on top of the line drawing and draw over the lines of the design with a soft pencil.

Preparing the mount (mat board)

Measure your finished embroidery and decide on the overall size of the mount. You may have a frame or an envelope that will dictate the size. Decide on the position of the embroidery within the mount. (Centring the design within the mount at top and sides or with more mount at the bottom usually looks best.) Remember to leave enough space for the painted border. Draw the measured area of your embroidery on the mounting card (mat board or stiff paper) in soft pencil using very straight precise lines. It is best to decorate the mount *before* cutting out the embroidery area.

To reproduce an identical border to the one shown in the photograph take a tracing from the outline printed on the page and transfer to the mount using dressmaker's carbon paper. The lines can be erased afterwards and so do not interfere with the colouring. You can, of course, draw your own border straight on to the mount using a soft pencil. Go over these lines with a black ink pen, erase pencil lines and then colour in.

If your embroidery is slightly different in size from the one in the book, for whatever reason, don't forget to alter the size of the border accordingly. Take this opportunity to add your own personal details to the mounts, making the pictures more individual.

If making a collage, paste stamps or coloured paper on to the mounting card before cutting out the overall area of the mount. Then cut out the overall size of mount followed by the inner embroidery area. This ensures the collage covers the whole mount evenly.

Cutting the mount (mat board)

Always use a sharp blade and ruler. Make your cut by using a few strokes along the pencil lines rather than one heavy one. This allows for better accuracy and gives a cleaner cut, especially at the corners.

Because the embroideries are generally small, and provided you are careful about keeping them square on the canvas, it is easy to mount them yourself. Remove the material from the stretcher frame and trim around the design, allowing about 1in (3cm) margin all around. Stick a strip of masking tape or sticky (transparent) tape, to the wrong side along the top of the embroidery half overlapping the edge of the fabric. Place the work right side up on a flat surface and position the mount also right side up so that the embroidery appears through the hole that you have cut for it. Press lightly so that the tape sticks to the back of the mount.

Once the top is in position, stick down the base of the picture in the same way, pulling the needlework tight and into shape. Attach the two remaining sides in the same way, gently pulling before sticking into place.

You can now use the mounted picture in a variety of ways, as suggested in the book; in clip frames, in moulded frames, or as book covers or greetings cards. If you are framing the design, cover it with glass to protect and preserve the stitches.

Note for North American readers

The measurements in this book are given in both inches and centimetres. Please note that the first measurement given is always the height and the second measurement is the width.

Adapting the designs

All the designs here are suitable for making other articles apart from pictures or cards. You can scale the design up or down to suit the article. You may also have to alter the stitch and/or thread accordingly. For example the ship design is worked in cross stitch for the cushion cover to give a more hardwearing texture. Straight stitches could pull or snag over a large area. The design remains the same because by following the chart you cover the same number of canvas threads. Each canvas thread covered by embroidery thread is one stitch, which translates to one cross stitch.

For embroidery designs you can stitch on any suitable items such as shirt pockets, pouch purses, cushion covers, pillow cases, tablecloths – the variations are endless.

$\mathcal{W}$ ELCOME HOME

A HOUSE PICTURE MAKES AN IDEAL PRESENT AT
ANY TIME BUT IS PERFECT FOR A
FRIEND WHO HAS JUST MOVED INTO A NEW HOME

Finished size

Embroidered picture 2½in × 2in (6.5cm × 5cm)

Materials

7in × 6in (18cm × 15cm) of 22-mesh canvas
Stranded cotton (floss): one skein each of sky blue, dark blue, light green, mid green, bright red, brick red, light brown, yellow, cream and white
Size 22 tapestry needle
Two bird-shaped sequins
Tiny beads
Invisible nylon thread
Fine needle for beading
Card (mat board) for mounting
Felt tips

Note: If you cannot find bird-shaped sequins, cut birds from fine cardboard or paper and use all-purpose adhesive to fix

Stitching

Use all six threads of the stranded cotton in the needle to sew the picture which is entirely worked in straight stitch. Follow the chart for the number of canvas threads the stitches cover.

Begin the design by following the bottom row of hearts. Then sew the base line of the border, turning from vertical to horizontal straight stitch at the corners, which are made neat by mitring. A diagonal stitch over the corner gives a tidy effect. Do not finish the sides and top of the border until the picture has been completed.

Stitch the picture by sewing the smaller and most central shapes first and then building up the surrounding areas. You can position the door in relation to the hearts by referring to the chart and follow on from there. The sky is the last area to stitch and you will find it is now easy to complete the border and the top row of hearts.

To suggest flowers and add a sparkle, sew beads on the lawn area with a fine needle and invisible thread. If you can't find tiny beads use French knots. Add bird sequins in the sky and straight stitch with two strands of cotton to suggest individual blades of grass on the lawn.

14

Mounting

When the tapestry is complete, mount it in card and add the decorative border.

The border you draw round your house picture can either be exactly as shown in the photograph or you can personalize it with little details conveying your own message.

For a wedding present add the names of the couple or the words Home Sweet Home.

$\flat$APPY BIRTHDAY

A CLOWN THAT WILL DELIGHT ANY CHILD – THE
ARC OF BALLS CLEVERLY LINKS THE EMBROIDERY
TO THE CIRCUS BORDER

Finished size
Embroidered picture 2in (5cm) square

Materials
7in (18cm) square of medium-weight calico (unbleached muslin)
Size 6 crewel needle
Stranded cotton (floss): one skein each of blue, white, pink, orange, magenta pink, green
Eight star sequins
Silver thread
Card (mat board) for mounting
Felt tips or crayons

Stitching
Trace the line drawing of the clown on to the fabric. Using all six strands of the thread begin by sewing the body of the clown, working outwards from the centre. Start with the centre stripe of blue, then work the white either side, followed by the blue outer stripes and the sleeves. By working outwards you avoid the problem of trying to squeeze in a stripe between two others. Note the clown's suit is worked in horizontal straight stitch, as shown by arrows on the diagram.

Now work the hands and face in pink, followed by the hat and shoes in magenta. Next sew the silver edges. Add the curls of hair using French knots worked in orange.

To make the eyes, work a loose French knot in white and make a blue French knot on top using a fine needle and only one strand of the cotton. Using two strands of magenta thread sew the mouth with one small straight stitch. Sew the sequins on to the cuffs, shoes, hat and suit front using large French knots (again with only one strand) to secure.

The clown makes an original birthday card or party invitation.

Mounting

Mount the embroidery in card and trace in the busy border. Colour in using felt tips or pens in vivid shades to suggest the circus atmosphere. The arc of balls carries the eye from the picture to the border.

The clown's suit can be
as subtle or vibrant as
you like. Here are a few
colour combinations for
inspiration.

*f*ORGET ME NOT

THEY SAY ELEPHANTS NEVER FORGET, SO THIS
PICTURE WOULD MAKE AN APPROPRIATE LEAVING
PRESENT TO GIVE A FRIEND GOING ABROAD

Finished size

Embroidered picture 4½in × 5¼in (11.5cm × 13.5cm)

Materials

9in (23cm) square heavy-weight calico (unbleached muslin)
Stranded cotton (floss): one skein each of grey, pink, purple, white, red, yellow
Size 6 crewel needle
Gold thread
Gold star sequins (approx 44)
Invisible nylon thread
Card (mat board) for mounting
Felt tips

Transfer the design to the fabric. You may find it easier to draw the circles using a compass and soft pencil or by drawing around circular objects.

Stitching

Start the embroidery by stitching the elephants' features. Sew the white tusks and eyes, then the pink of the ears and toes. Finally, fill in the grey bodies, all in vertical straight stitch.

The elephants' blankets are worked in trellis stitch by first sewing diagonal lines of gold thread across the blanket area. Where the gold threads cross, sew an upright cross stitch to secure the threads, using three strands of red thread. In each diamond-shaped space make a purple French knot. Also with purple, make one stitch across each eye. Using three strands of yellow, sew a line of chain stitch around the edge of the blankets.

Sew the star-spangled circles by starting with the inner circle and working outwards. Use straight stitch and alter the angle of the stitches (see arrows on diagram) as you work so that they radiate out from the centre and there are no gaps. At the same time, sew each band on the striped ball.

When the circles are finished, sew lines of back stitches along the joins and outer edges using gold thread. With invisible thread sew on the star sequins, spacing them evenly over the circles and placing one on the ball.

Mounting

Mount the embroidery and decorate the border with random groups of five-pointed stars. Colour them with felt tips in shades to complement the threads.

A design like this one works well with a variety of animals.   *Choose one with a shape that works well as a mirror image.*

HAPPY DAYS

FLOAT UP, UP AND AWAY WITH THIS MAGICAL
TRIO OF PICTURES COMBINING THE SKILLS OF
EMBROIDERY AND PAINTING

Finished size

Large embroidered picture 6¾in × 3¾in (17cm × 9.5cm)
Small pictures 2½in × 2in (5cm × 6.5cm)

Materials

11in × 8in (28cm × 20cm) heavy-weight calico (unbleached muslin)
Embroidery hoop or frame
Stranded cotton (floss): one skein each of white, brown, yellow, red, pink, orange, gold, blue, green, violet
Size 5 crewel needle
Tapestry, crewel or fine knitting yarn in various colours for landscape
Thick black thread
Water-based felt tips, inks or paints
Card (mat board) for mounting

Stitching

Measure out the area of the embroidered picture on to the fabric and trace the line drawing through the fabric to give you the outlines of the picture. It is not necessary to draw the rope lines as these can easily be sewn on the finished picture. A helpful hint is to use a coin or round object to draw around to achieve a neat shape for the sun and balloons.

Stretch out the canvas on a frame or embroidery hoop. If felt tips are to be used, lightly apply the different sky colours in short strokes and then, with a wet paint brush, blend the colours together by 'washing' with brush and water.

If using inks, again wash over the canvas with the different colours, allowing them to blend together. The more the inks are diluted with water, the paler they become. It is not necessary to avoid painting on the areas to be embroidered as these will be sewn over.

Before sewing, allow the canvas to dry thoroughly otherwise the thread may get stained. Begin by stitching the stripes of the balloons, one balloon at a time. Start with the top colour and work each stripe in order, always working down into the previous stitches, rather than coming up and pulling out the previous stitches. Keep the stitches very straight, working shorter stitches at the sides to achieve the smooth curve of the balloon.

Use the colours to maximum impact so that the balloons are really vibrant. When the

Here the designs are smaller than life-size. Use the photos overleaf when working the embroidery.

To gain confidence with this picture you may want to practise with just one balloon and work the pictures individually as here.

balloons are complete, sew the baskets using brown cotton. Next join the baskets to sides and base of the balloon using black thread. Work the sun and clouds in vertical straight stitch.

For the landscape, sew on the various colours of the fields, one at a time, starting at the top. To suggest a river at the base of the picture, some of the blue stranded cotton has been used. Add a carpet of colourful flowers worked in French knots with the same cottons used for the balloons.

These smaller pictures can be displayed next to the larger one, to suggest more balloons floating into the sky.

Mounting

Mount the completed embroidery and continue the image created in stitches on to the mount by using paints in a wash technique. Define the continuation of the clouds by painting the blue sky around it – a faint blue crayon line may help. Continue the colours of the landscape by painting complementary colours on either side. Use crayons or felt tips to allow the colourful flowers to pour out on to the mount.

CONGRATULATIONS

CELEBRATE A WEDDING WITH THIS PERMANENT
KEEPSAKE OF THE DAY. CHOOSE THE COLOURS OF
THE DRESS AND HAIR TO SUIT THE REAL BRIDE

Finished size

Embroidered picture 2¾in × 2¼in (7cm × 5.5cm)

Materials

7in × 6in (18cm × 15cm) of 22-mesh canvas
Size 22 tapestry needle
Stranded cotton (floss): one skein each of sky blue, white, black, dark grey, brown, red, four shades of green
Sewing thread: a few lengths each of red and blue
Two bird-shaped sequins
Tiny beads
Fine needle for beading
Invisible nylon thread
Multi-coloured sparkling thread (use gold or silver if not available)
Card (mat board) for mounting
Felt tips or crayons

The colours of the beads are random, but they could be chosen to match the colour scheme of the wedding or, for an anniversary present, kept to gold, silver or ruby.

Stitching

Using all six strands of the thread, sew the pink hands and faces in vertical straight stitch following the chart carefully to make sure the positions are correct. Sew the facial features using red and blue thread.

Then sew the white areas following the chart for straight stitch lengths and noting that the man's cuffs are worked horizontally. When using white thread, keep the length of thread quite short, as a long thread could get dirty and spoil the finished picture.

Next sew the grey areas – the man's shoes, jacket collar and lapels, and the hat band. Complete the suit and hat with black thread.

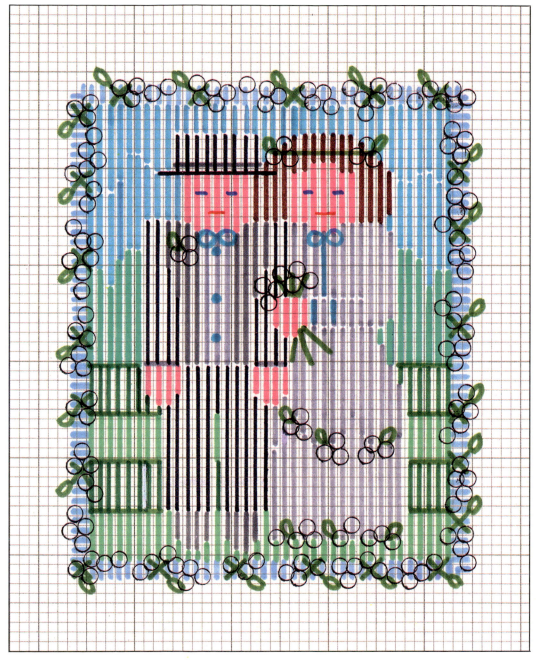

Sew the bride's hair in brown, or in a colour to suit the real bride. Fill in the sky area and, while you have blue thread in the needle, make the French knots for the man's shirt buttons and add a few straight stitches on her dress – 'something blue' for good luck – and daisy stitches for bows.

Using green, sew the bushes and lawn. Next sew a border around the picture in sparkling thread to frame the design. Add a trellis of straight and daisy stitches to the border. Sew flowers of beads to the trellis, using invisible thread so that the sparkling thread shows through subtly. Alternatively, use French knots for the flowers.

Using green thread and more beads or French knots, sew the bride's headdress, bouquet and skirt decoration, plus the man's buttonhole.

Mounting

When the embroidery is complete, mount it on card and draw the floral border to echo the colours in the picture. Add the couple's names, date and any other wedding details at the top.

HAPPY HOLIDAYS

A SAILING SHIP SET FOR THE FOUR WINDS,
IN A SEA OF STAMPS, EVOKES THE MEMORY OF
TRAVEL TO EXOTIC FARAWAY PLACES

Finished size

Embroidered picture 2¾in × 1¾in (7cm × 4.5cm)

Materials

7in × 6in (18cm × 15cm) of 22-mesh canvas
Size 22 tapestry needle
Stranded cotton (floss): one skein each of white, pale pink, pale blue, mid brown, dark brown, six contrasting shades of blue for sea
Gold thread
Thick black cotton thread
Tiny beads: blue, mauve and gold
Two bird sequins
Invisible nylon thread
Card (mat board) for mounting
Fine needle for beading

Stitching

Begin by stitching the small areas first, such as the windows of the ship. Using all six strands of the dark brown thread, and following the chart for position, work windows in vertical straight stitch. Then work the rest of the ship in mid brown. Now work the main sail and pennant in white and the front sail in pale pink.

Next work the sun in gold, being careful to keep a neat round shape. Fill in the background sky with staggered straight stitches to suggest clouds.

To create the muted colours in the sea, make up your own six-stranded thread by taking one strand from each of the six shades of blue and lightly twisting them together to form a subtle blend of colours. Use this unique thread to sew the sea in staggered straight stitches to suggest rolling waves. It is not essential to follow the chart here as long as care is taken to develop smooth, flowing waves.

Add sparkle to the crashing sea by sewing beads along the lines of the waves. Alternatively make clusters of French knots worked in single colours and gold.

Add the mast and rope in black thread, taking care not to pull the stitches too tight, or leave them too loose. Sew on bird sequins with invisible thread.

Mounting

When the embroidery is complete, mount it on card and cover the border with a collage of colourful stamps to create an exciting pattern reflecting the theme of travel. A double border of white and blue (stiff) cartridge paper allows the embroidery to stand out from the border.

The photograph shows the design slightly smaller than life-size. Use the photo overleaf when working the embroidery.

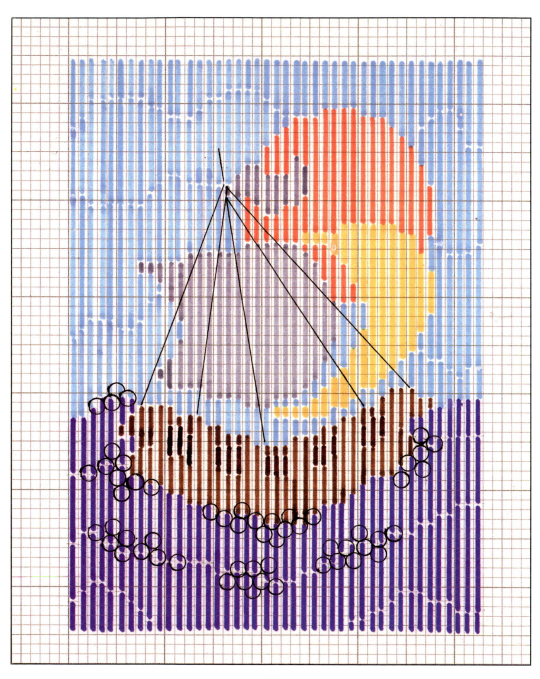

If this is to be a Bon
Voyage present, the
border could be
personalized by
selecting stamps only
from the country of
destination.

You can easily adapt
the design to make
three cushions using
cross stitch on 10-mesh
canvas and stranded
wool. The sea has been
worked in bands of
different blues,
interspersed with white
to suggest the surf.

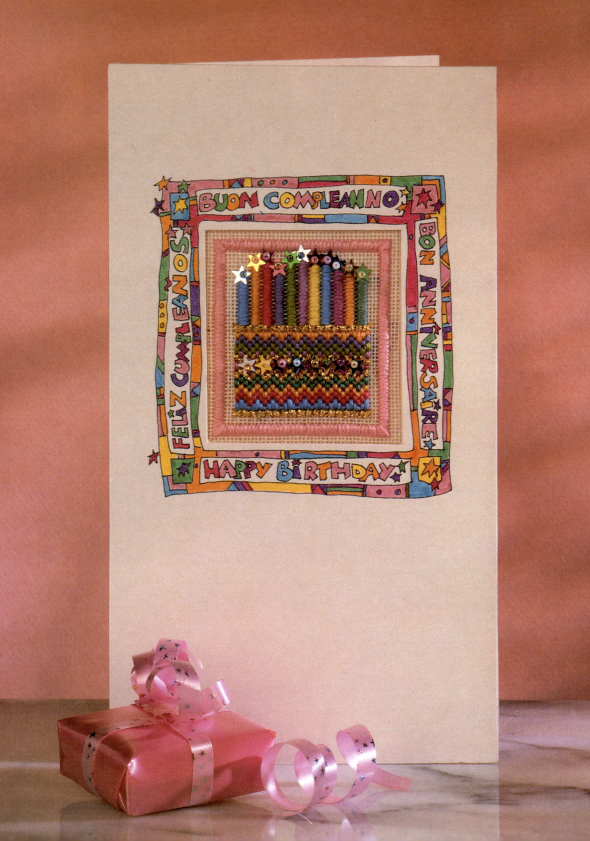

MANY HAPPY RETURNS

A TRULY INTERNATIONAL BIRTHDAY PRESENT THAT CAN BE ADAPTED TO SUIT ANY AGE BY CHANGING THE NUMBER OF CANDLES ON THE CAKE

Finished size
Embroidered picture 2½in × 2in (6.5cm × 5cm)

Materials
7in × 6in (18cm × 15cm) of 22-mesh canvas
Size 22 tapestry needle
Stranded cotton (floss): various colours
Gold thread
Star sequins: various colours
Tiny beads
Invisible nylon thread
Fine needle for beading
Card (stiff paper) for mounting
Felt tips or crayons

The birthday card is shown slightly smaller than life size.

Stitching
Use all six strands of the thread in the needle to sew the picture. The candles are worked in horizontal straight stitch, the cake in vertical stitches. The top and the base of the cake are worked in cross stitch using gold thread.

Begin the design by stitching the candles from left to right, over three canvas threads. Take care to insert the needle down into the hole used for the previous candle rather than coming up and pulling the previous thread. Vary the height of each candle to add interest.

When the candles are complete, stitch the cake pattern starting at the top near the candles with a row of cross stitch worked in gold thread. Work each cross stitch over two canvas threads and extend the line beyond the candles by one stitch at either end.

Continue to work the cake in vertical straight stitch, one row at a time. Vary the colours to reflect the colours of the candles, and add a line of gold thread across the centre. Finish at the base of the cake with a second row of cross stitch in gold.

Add a star sequin to each candle, secured with a bead, using invisible thread. Sew the remaining sequins and beads across the centre of the cake.

Add a border of vertical and horizontal straight stitch to frame the design, 'mitring' the corners as shown.

Mounting

Draw in the colourful 'Happy Birthday' mosaic using felt tips or crayons in shades to complement the cake and candles. Alternatively, choose just one of the four international greetings and use the remaining three sides to add the date and name of the special person.

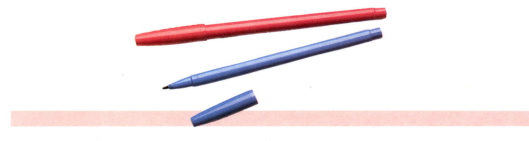

BUON NATALE

FELIZ NAVIDAD

JOYEUX NOËL

HAPPY CHRISTMAS

You could also adapt the birthday cake design to a Christmas cake by adding an extra candle – for the twelve days of Christmas – and working the embroidery in red, gold, white and green. You will need to make the cake slightly wider to make room for the extra candle.

hAPPY MEMORIES

CELEBRATE THE BIRTH OF A BABY WITH
TRADITIONAL KNITTED BOOTEES. ADD THE
BABY'S NAME, DATE AND WEIGHT TO MAKE THE
PRESENT MORE PERSONAL

Finished size

Each embroidered picture 2in (5cm) square

Materials

6in (15cm) square heavy-weight calico (unbleached muslin)

Tapestry, crewel or fine knitting wool in colour of your choice

Size 6 crewel needle

Stranded cotton (floss): one skein each of grey and colour to match bootees

Silver thread

Card (mat board) for mounting

Felt tips or crayons

Sew just one pair of bootees, if preferred, or two for twins. You can either make a picture or punch holes in the card, thread a ribbon through and make a photo album.

Stitching

Draw the bootee design on to the fabric. Following the diagram, stitch the knitting needles in straight stitches using grey thread. Work a line of silver stitches to add sparkle and make the needles look more realistic.

Using one strand of yarn, sew the loose end of the ball of yarn in back stitch. Then working from the left, stitch the bootees from the needles towards the feet using open chain stitch. Make the chain stitches more open at the top and tighter at the feet. This is achieved by making a smaller loop, bringing the needle closer to the previous stitch and pulling the thread slightly tighter. In this way, the shape of the baby bootees is formed giving a very realistic impression of knitting.

Using three strands of thread in a colour to match, define the base of the bootees in back stitch and add daisy loops to represent bows.

Mounting

Mount the picture and extend the visual image of the yarn continuing on to the border by drawing loops or a ball of yarn using felt tips or crayons.

Use this photograph as a guide when working the embroidery; the photo on the previous page shows the design smaller than life size.

t H A N K Y O U

THIS SIMPLE ARRANGEMENT OF FRUIT, FLOWERS
AND WINE MAKES A PERFECT THANK YOU
PRESENT FOR A SPECIAL DINNER PARTY

Finished size
Embroidered picture 2¼in × 2in (5.5cm × 5cm)

Materials
6in (15cm) square of 22-mesh canvas
Size 22 tapestry needle
Stranded cotton (floss): one skein each of burgundy red, white, bottle green, leaf green, orange, apple red, yellow/green, brown, pale blue, pink, purple, violet, pale green, cream, and three pale colours for tablecloth
Tiny beads: purple for grapes, plus other colours
Invisible nylon thread
Card (stiff paper) for mounting
Fine needle for beading

Stitching
Using six strands of thread throughout, begin at the centre of the chart with the bowl of fruit and build your picture outwards. Stitch one colour at a time following the chart for stitch lengths.

Be careful to make the long stitches of the tablecloth the right tensions to prevent sagging or puckering.

Please see overleaf for the chart and life-size picture.

Make the bunch of grapes by sewing on the purple beads with invisible thread. Sew a few of the coloured beads on to the flower arrangement.

Mounting
When the embroidery is complete, mount it in card, leaving room for a personal message.

Celebrate the harvest with this picture of nature's bounty. It would make a thoughtful present for a keen gardener at Thanksgiving or Harvest Festival.

fOR MY VALENTINE

A QUICK AND EASY EMBROIDERY TO WISH LOTS
OF LOVE ON VALENTINE'S DAY, A WEDDING
ANNIVERSARY OR JUST TO SAY THANK YOU

Finished size
Embroidered picture 2in (5cm) square

Materials
6in (15cm) square 22-mesh canvas
Stranded cotton (floss): one skein each of pink and green
Size 22 (tapestry) needle
80 coloured beads
Invisible nylon thread
Fine needle for beading
Card (stiff paper) for mounting
Crayons and fine black pen

Stitching
Following the chart, work the rows of hearts in vertical straight stitch, using all six strands of the pink embroidery thread. Using three strands of green thread, sew the cross stitch border and the crosses in between the hearts.

Sew on the coloured beads with invisible thread, spacing ten along each side of the border and four beads around each cross stitch within the picture.

Mounting
Mount your sewn picture in card and draw in the border as shown with a fine black pen. Crayon the design in soft colours to match the embroidery and beads.

Rows of tiny repeated hearts would adapt well to make a sweet pin cushion or herb sachet.

50

gREETINGS FOR BABY

FORGET ABOUT THE SLEEPLESS NIGHTS... THIS PICTURE OF A CONTENTED BABY IN A CRIB WILL MAKE A DELIGHTFUL BIRTHDAY OR CHRISTENING PRESENT

Finished size

Embroidered picture 4¼in × 2¾in (11cm × 7cm)

Materials

9in × 7in (23cm × 18cm) heavy-weight calico (unbleached muslin)
Size 6 crewel needle
Stranded cotton (floss): one skein each of white, pale yellow, pink, pale blue, mauve, pale green
Thin grey thread
Thin red thread
Thin brown yarn
Embroidery hoop or frame
Card (mat board) for mounting
Pink felt tips/inks/pastel crayons

Stitching

Trace the outline of the baby and cot on to the fabric. Stretch the fabric over the embroidery hoop or frame. Paint the pink areas of the baby's face and hands, being careful at the edges. Once the ink or felt tip has dried begin the embroidery.

Using all six strands of thread, sew the yellow baby's bonnet and white nightgown in vertical straight stitch. Sew the ribbon bows around the edge of the cot, either in one colour or in various pastel shades as shown. Use straight stitch both vertically and horizontally to define the shape of the bows (see arrows on diagram).

To give the baby's face and hands definition, sew along the traced outline in tiny back stitches worked in grey thread. Do the same using red thread for the mouth.

For the blanket, use trellis stitch and white thread to sew long stitches diagonally across the cover from one side to the other. Work in one direction at a time and space the lines evenly. Where each set of white threads cross, sew a vertical cross stitch in one of the pastel colours to hold the long threads in place. Finally, inside each diamond-shaped space, make a French knot in pale green. Also in green, add a bow under the baby's chin by sewing two daisy stitches and leaving two loose threads.

For the baby's curls, sew loose French knots around the baby's bonnet in brown yarn, or shade to suit the baby's colouring. Also in brown yarn, sew chain stitches around the edge of the crib to suggest basketweave.

Mounting

Mount the embroidery in a white border. Draw in the bold geometric pattern and, using the same colours as the threads, lightly crayon in the shapes to complement the delicacy of the embroidery. Leave a space at the base of the border to include the baby's name and birthdate.

bAPPY EASTER

**MAKE A HIGHLY INDIVIDUAL EASTER CARD OR
SIMPLY WELCOME SPRING WITH A
SHEEP GRAZING IN A MEADOW OF FLOWERS**

Finished size
Embroidered picture 3in (7.5cm) square

Materials
7in (18cm) square of heavy-weight calico
(unbleached muslin)
Embroidery hoop or frame
Stranded cotton (floss): one skein each of
magenta, red, bright yellow, lemon yellow,
green, turquoise green, turquoise blue, violet,
three shades of green for grass
Size 5 crewel needle
Coloured beads
Invisible nylon thread
Fine needle for beading
Black silk thread
White knitting yarn
Two bird sequins
Card (stiff paper) for mounting
Blue inks/felt tips

Stitching
Trace the drawing of the sheep on to the fabric.
It is easier to draw the border of geometric
shapes directly on to the fabric using pencil and
ruler.

To paint the sky, stretch out the calico on a
frame or embroidery hoop. If using felt tips,
lightly apply the sky colour in short strokes and
then with a wet paintbrush blend the strokes
together by 'washing' with brush and water. If
using ink, simply 'wash' the fabric with the
diluted ink. When the fabric has dried, sew the
legs and head of the sheep in horizontal straight
stitch, using black thread.

To sew the grass, take two strands from each
of the three greens and mix together to give the
effect of the contrasting shades in grass. Using
scattered straight stitches of random lengths,
fill in the grassed area.

Using one strand of white yarn, fill in the
sheep's body with French knots sewn fairly
loosely to suggest fleece. Sew on two white
beads for eyes or make tight French knots using
the same white yarn. Add yellow beads or
French knots to the grass to suggest spring
flowers.

Sew the squares of the border in vertical
straight stitch, evenly distributing the colours

around the edge. It may be easier to sew the inner row of squares first, followed by the outer row. The squares do not necessarily have to be perfect squares. An uneven effect adds to the simple charm of the design.

Mounting

To create an even more colourful image, decorate the mount with a border of various geometric shapes using felt tips or crayons in the same shades as the stitched border.

Scatter small sheep all over a piece of fabric and make up into a highly original cushion.

MERRY CHRISTMAS

SEND SEASONAL GREETINGS TO SPECIAL FRIENDS AND FAMILY WITH THIS SIMPLE CROSS-STITCH CHRISTMAS TREE STREWN WITH DECORATIONS

Finished size of Christmas card

Embroidered picture approx 3in (7.5cm) square

Materials

9in (23cm) square of 10-mesh canvas
3-stranded yarn: one skein each of green, red and brown
Size 18 tapestry needle
Approx 17 metallic beads
Invisible nylon thread
Fine needle for beading
Card (stiff paper) for mounting
Felt tips or crayons

Stitching

Using all three strands of green and brown yarn, work the tree shape and the tub in cross-stitch, making sure the upper threads of each cross lie in the same direction.

Using three strands of red, work the cross-stitch border around the tree and add a sash to the top of the tub by working a straight stitch and a daisy stitch for the bow.

Add large metallic beads in scale with the tree to represent decorations. Write your personal message on a small tag and stitch it carefully on to the pot with some red yarn.

Mounting

Mount the picture and add a decorative border of festive designs using colourful felt tips.

Finished size of gift tag

Approx 1½in (4cm) square

Materials

6in (15cm) square of 22-mesh canvas
Size 22 tapestry needle
Stranded cotton (floss): one skein each of red, green and brown
Beads: bugle and round
One star sequin
Invisible nylon thread
Fine needle
Card (stiff paper) for mounting

Stitching

Using all six strands of the thread, work the tree shape and tub in cross stitch, making sure all the upper threads of each cross lie in the same direction.

Using three strands of red thread, work the

cross stitch border around the tree. Add a sash to the top of the tub by working a straight stitch and a daisy stitch for the bow.

Add glitter and sparkle by decorating the tree with bugle beads for crackers (Christmas party favors) and round beads for baubles, sewn on with invisible thread. Top the tree with a star sequin.

Mounting

Mount the finished picture in a small piece of card for a gift tag. Cut out the hole for the picture as close to the red border as possible. Keep the tag plain to make the simple tree design even more effective.

This is the border for
the Christmas card.

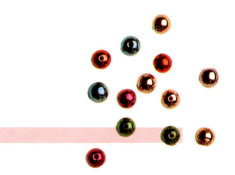

You can adapt the design for a cushion by arranging rows of trees in a symmetrical design. The chart shows a possible arrangement on 10-mesh canvas with each square representing one cross stitch in stranded wool. The trees on the cushion are the same size as the tree on the Christmas card.

$\mathcal{W}$ITH LOVE

LAY THE TABLE FOR TEA WITH A FLOWER-
SPRIGGED CLOTH AND MATCHING CHINA. A
DELIGHTFUL PRESENT FOR A COTTAGE-
STYLE HOME

Finished size
Embroidered picture 3in (7.5cm) square

Materials
7in (18cm) square of 22-mesh canvas
Stranded cotton (floss): one skein each of blue,
white, pale green, pink
Gold thread
Size 22 tapestry needle
Card (mat board) for mounting
Felt tips or crayons

Stitching
The design is worked in tent stitch using three
strands of thread throughout. Following the
chart, sew the outline of the teapot, cup and
saucer in continental tent stitch using the gold
thread.

The next stage is to stitch the flowers on the
china and cloth, using the chart as a guide or by
sewing them at random. To sew the flowers
begin by working the white centres, then the
pale pink and green. Using blue thread fill in
the area of the pot, cup and saucer and then sew
the diagonal lines around the border. (Use
Basketweave tent stitch for the border.) Leave
the area behind the teapot, cup and saucer
blank. Fill in this area later with white thread to
set off the china. Complete the rest of the
patterned border in Basketweave tent stitch
with white thread.

*This design looks very
effective when worked
on a larger mesh canvas
with thicker thread.*

Mounting

Mount the finished picture in a white border, cutting the frame as close to the stitching as possible. Draw in the blue lines around the edges using a ruler. Add a scattering of pink flowers to complement the embroidery.

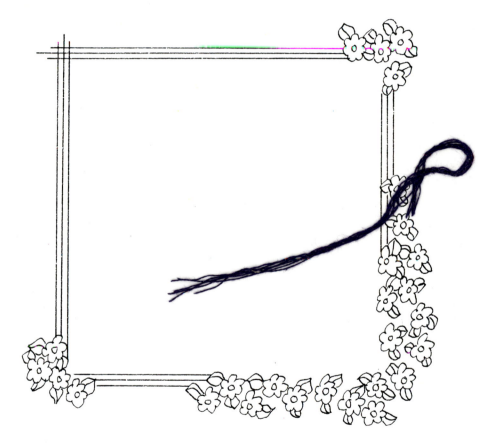

gET WELL SOON

CAPTURE THE BEAUTY OF THE CHANGING
SEASONS WITH THIS SAMPLE LANDSCAPE SEEN
THROUGH A WINDOW. EMBROIDER JUST ONE
SEASON OR THE WHOLE YEAR

Finished size

Each embroidered picture 2½in (6cm) square

Materials

22-mesh canvas:
7in (18cm) square for one season
12in (30cm) square for all four seasons
Size 22 tapestry needle
Stranded cotton (floss), one skein each as follows:
Summer two shades of blue, three shades of green, orange/yellow, brown, pale yellow.
Spring two shades of blue, white, yellow, four shades of green, brown.
Autumn blue/green, pale mauve, two chestnut browns, three shades of brown, green, ochre yellow.
Winter pale violet, white, grey, creamy white, brown, dark blue, two shades of green.

Coloured beads
Invisible nylon thread
Fine needle for beading
Card (mat board) for mounting
Wrapping paper or wallpaper
Cartridge (good quality drawing) paper
Glue
Fine black felt tip

Stitching

If you want to sew all four pictures at once, leave plenty of space around each picture while stitching. They can then be cut up and mounted closer together in the window frame.

Using vertical straight stitch throughout and all six strands of thread, follow the charts to sew the landscapes. It is simpler to begin with the foreground of each picture and work up to the sky. Be careful when working long stitches, such as for the trees and winter sky, to keep the threads taut.

Mounting

These landscapes are mounted in a window frame as if it were the view from the convalescent's window. To add to this idea, the window frame is surrounded by a real wallpaper border. The contrast between the wallpaper and the black and white window frame sets off the colours and graphic design of the landscapes.

First select a suitable wallpaper or wrapping paper. (You could use some spare wallpaper from the room where the picture will hang.) Glue the paper on to the mounting card.

Depending on the size of your landscapes and how many you have done, draw a window frame

like the one shown in the photograph with a fine black felt tip on to a piece of cartridge paper. Draw the area(s) of embroidery inside the frame in pencil. Carefully cut around the outer black line of the frame and stick the window drawing on top of the wallpaper,

SPRING

centring it over the design. Once it is positioned, follow the pencil lines and cut out the areas for embroidery through the cartridge paper, wallpaper and card all at once. Place the embroideries in position.

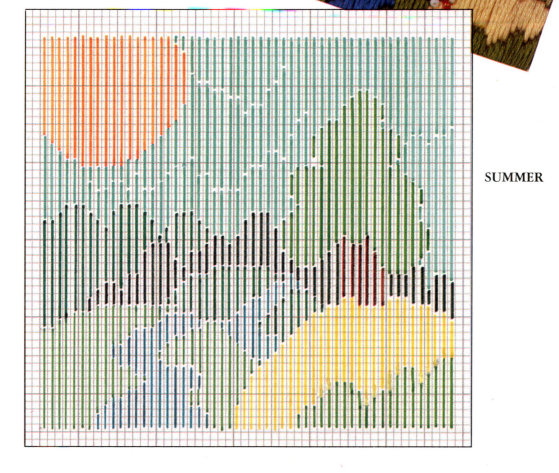

SUMMER

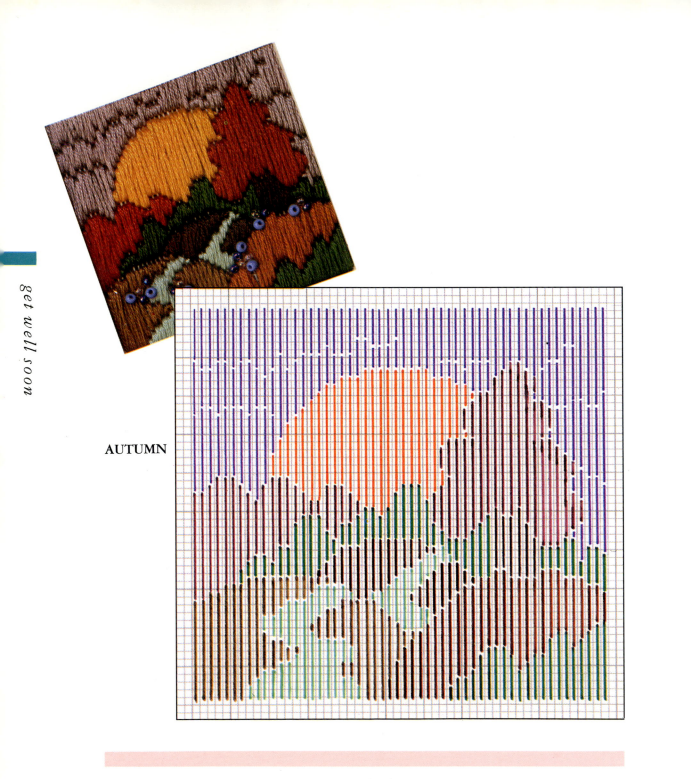

AUTUMN

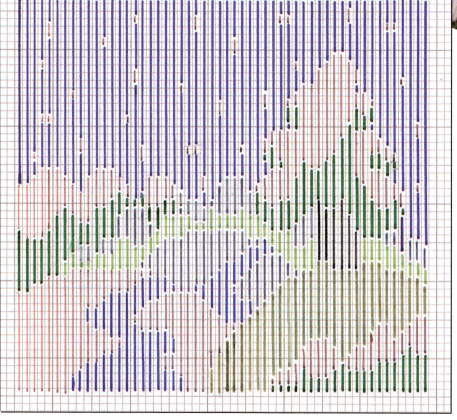

WINTER

hAPPY ANNIVERSARY

SEND FLOWERS TO SOMEONE SPECIAL WITH A
MESSAGE OF YOUR LOVE, INSPIRED BY THE SONG
'PLANT YOUR LOVE AND LET IT GROW'

Finished size

Embroidered picture 2½in (6.5cm) square

Materials

7in (18cm) square of 22-mesh canvas
Size 22 tapestry needle
Sparkling thread: blue and gold
Fine tapestry yarn: brown
Stranded cotton (floss): one skein each of
yellow, three shades of pink
Coton perlé (pearl cotton) 5: two shades of
green
Tiny beads
Invisible nylon thread
Fine needle for beading
Light card or paper for tag
Card (mat board) for mounting
Felt-tips and fine black pen

Stitching

Measure out the square 'window' area on to
canvas and draw the outline of the sun by
drawing around a coin using a soft pencil or pale
felt tip. Alternatively follow the chart. (This
design looks equally effective stitched in
embroidery on fabric.)

Using all six strands of thread throughout,
sew the sun in straight stitch in yellow. Be
careful to get the right tension to prevent
sagging or pulling.

Following the chart, stitch a plant pot in
brown tapestry wool, centring the pot along the
base of the window. Sew the window frame in
cross stitch using gold thread.

Now stitch the hearts in the three different
shades of pink thread, following the chart for
position, if wished. Join the hearts together
with small straight stitches worked in green
cotton to represent foliage. Add more green
stitches to the window frame to suggest trellis.

*This sunny picture
could also be adapted to
make an original
Mother's Day present.*

Sew the beads amongst the hearts and also around the border to echo the design, using invisible thread. Stitch streaks of blue sparkling thread to suggest the glitter of glass.

Add the finishing touch by writing your personal message on a tiny tag of card and sewing it to the pot with pink thread.

Mounting

Mount the picture in card and draw in the border as shown with a fine black pen. Colour the design with felt-tips.

Use this line drawing if you are working the design in embroidery.

79

hAPPY NEW YEAR

TRANSLATE A FAVOURITE WATERCOLOUR OR
POSTCARD INTO FREESTYLE EMBROIDERY AND
ENJOY EXPERIMENTING WITH THE USE OF
COLOUR

Finished size
Will depend on size of subject

Materials
Postcard, photograph or painting
Tracing paper
22-mesh canvas
Stranded cotton (floss): various colours
Size 22 tapestry needle
Tiny beads
Invisible nylon thread
Fine needle for beading
Card (mat board) for mounting
Felt tips or crayons

Note: There is no chart for this picture because the beauty of the design is in the freedom of interpreting the scene in your own colours.

Stitching
Take a favourite postcard, photograph or painting, lay the tracing paper on top and draw lines over the image to divide it crudely into blocks of colour.

Choose as few colours as possible to work the embroidery so that shapes of colours are formed and the landscape image is retained. Using the horizontal lines as contours, work the design in vertical straight stitches. Add texture with beads sewn on with invisible thread – here they suggest the sparkling surf where the sea meets the shore.

This style of embroidery allows you to discover the joys of using colour and the effect colours have in relation to each other. Experiment with colours to create a balanced and harmonious landscape. You can take the colour

scheming further and enlarge the embroidery until the design becomes almost totally abstract.

Mounting

Mount your finished embroidery, then draw in the contemporary border of random shapes and colour using felt tips or crayons in shades to reflect and balance the picture.

This is the original watercolour which inspired the tapestry.

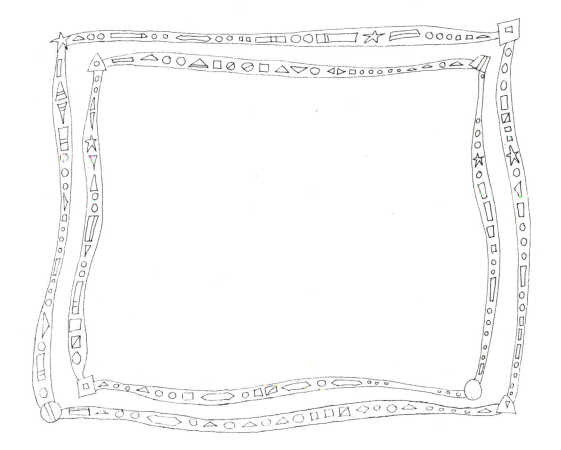

This detail of the design shows the beads which represent the sparkle of the surf.

f OR MOTHER, WITH LOVE

A VASE OF TULIPS SUGGESTS SPRINGTIME OCCASIONS SUCH AS MOTHER'S DAY OR EASTER, PICK YOUR FAVOURITE COLOURS FOR THIS TIMELESS ARRANGEMENT

Finished size

Embroidered picture 5½in (14cm) square

Materials

10in (25cm) square 18-mesh canvas
Stranded cotton (floss): five skeins white, one skein each of two shades of red, two shades of green, one skein each of purple, pale blue, yellow
Size 20 tapestry needle
Card (mat board) for mounting
Felt tips

Trace the line drawing of the tulip design directly on to the canvas. Measure out the area for the background and borders with a pencil and ruler.

Stitching

Following the chart, sew the tulips, leaves and vase in Continental or half-cross tent stitch.

Now add the butterflies in the corners, as here, or at random if preferred. To stitch the central background, work in white diagonal stitches over two and three canvas intersections with coloured rows of tent stitch in between. (This stitch is based on the basketweave method.)

For the spotted border, sew the spots first by stitching coloured squares randomly over the border area. Fill in the border with white using the basketweave method as much as possible. Work the outer border by sewing diagonal stripes of basketweave tent stitch using all the colours of the main picture.

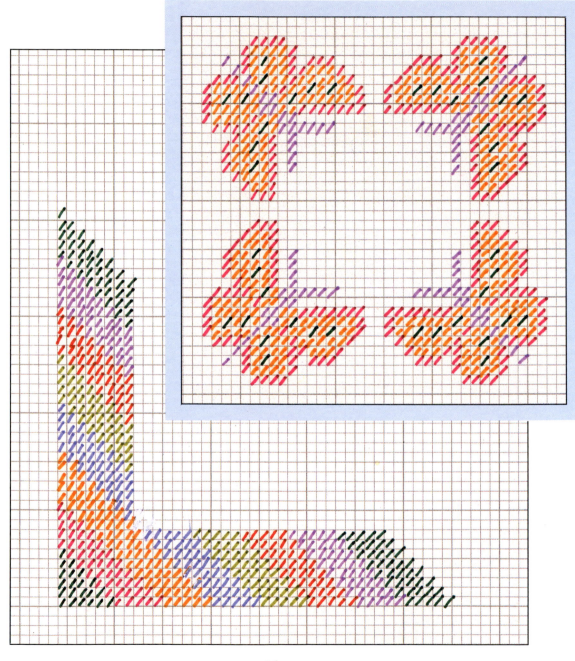

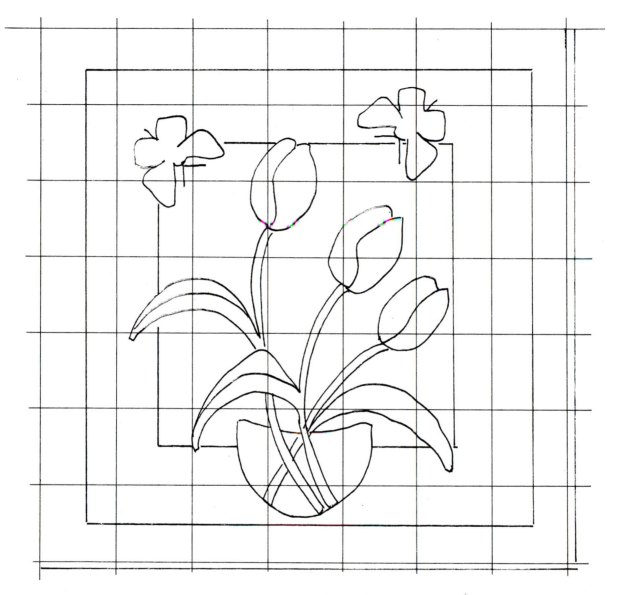

for mother, with love

Mounting
Mount the design in white card and dot with
coloured felt tips to echo the sewn border.

f OR FATHER, WITH LOVE

THIS COLOURFUL EMBROIDERY IS GREAT FOR USING UP ODDMENTS OF THREAD. IT MAKES A FUN DESIGN TO GIVE A DOODLE-CRAZY FATHER

Finished size
Embroidered picture 3in (7.5cm) square

Materials
7in (18cm) square 18-mesh canvas
Stranded cotton (floss): three skeins of white, oddments of red, green, turquoise, yellow, purple, dark blue
Size 20 tapestry needle
Card (stiff paper) for mounting
Crayons
Tracing or tissue paper
Coins
Paper glue

Note: There is no chart for the border as it is made from coin rubbings.

Stitching
You can either follow the illustrated design stitch by stitch, or mark out your own square and draw in squiggles to fill the area. A personalized picture could be made by taking a friend's page of doodles and interpreting them in embroidery.

Stitch the squiggles in Continental tent stitch using all six strands of thread. Try to balance the colours evenly over the canvas. When the design is complete, fill in the background with the main colour, working the tent stitch in the basketweave method wherever possible.

Mounting
This colourful border is made from coin rubbings worked on lightweight tracing or tissue paper. Choose crayons to complement the colours of the embroidery threads. Glue the border to the mounting card and cut out the centre for the design.

gOOD LUCK

A BRIGHT, CHEERFUL DESIGN WHERE THE
COLOURS OF THE MAT ARE COMPLEMENTED BY
THE BOLD BLACK AND WHITE CAT. A MUST FOR
CAT LOVERS

Finished size

Embroidered picture 3in × 3½in (8cm × 9cm), including fringe

Materials

9in × 10in (23cm × 25cm) medium-weight calico (unbleached muslin)

Size 6 crewel needle

Stranded cotton (floss): one skein each of black, white, pink, pale green, various colours for the rug

Gold thread

Sequin stars

Tiny beads

Invisible nylon thread

Fine needle for beading

Card (stiff paper) for mounting

Felt tips or crayons

Note: This design is stitched on to calico (unbleached muslin), although none of the fabric shows. It can easily be adapted for 22-mesh canvas and the diamond shapes of the rug would then become more regular.

Stitching

Begin by tracing the outline of the design on to the fabric. Sew the eyes, nose and pink of the ears first. Then sew the white shapes of the cat, taking care to make even contours to define the arch of the back, legs and paws. Using the black thread sew the rest of the cat. Use split stitch where the black and white meet each other so that they blend together as they would in fur. Finally, sew the remaining pink areas of the paws and add the gold sparkle of the cat's eyes and whiskers.

Develop the pattern of the rug by sewing the diamond shapes nearest to the cat and working outwards to fill the rectangle. Try to distribute the colours of the rug attractively and take care not to use very dark colours around the cat so that the shape of the cat does not get lost. You could plan the arrangement on paper first.

Make straight stitches, at least ½in (1cm) long, around the edge of the rug to make the fringe. Use as much thread as required, randomly stitching in one colour at a time until the border is densely filled.

Sew stars around the edge, securing them with tiny beads. Finally cut the long stitches of the border to create the fringe effect.

Change the colours to suit your own décor – or your cat.

Mounting

If mounting the design in card, cut the hole in the card smaller than the overall size of the rug, so that the fringe is raised slightly and rests on top, covering the cut edges. Draw in the geometric border and colour in with felt tips or crayons

*It could also be used to
make a pin cushion,
replacing the beads
with coloured glass-
headed pins to decorate.*

EMBROIDERY STITCHES

1 Back stitch
A basic stitch for outlining and defining shapes. Make the stitch by working one stitch forward, two stitches back (underneath) to form a continuous line of small stitches. It uses a lot of thread on the reverse side.

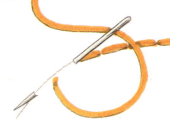

2 Split stitch
Use this stitch for outlining or filling in a large flat area. It uses less thread than back stitch and gives a flatter but thicker outline. It is also

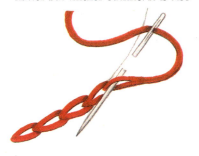

good for blending two colours together to avoid a hard line, as in the picture of the black and white cat. After making a small forward stitch, take a small back stitch on the same line and bring the needle up through the previous stitch, splitting the thread.

3 Straight stitch
Straight stitch is one single spaced stitch used singly, or as a filling stitch. Make each stitch to any length in any direction.

4 Satin stitch
This is similar to straight stitch but worked in parallel lines, close together, to cover an area completely. You need to take care at the edge to form a good line. Do not make the stitches too long or pull

the thread too tight as this will pucker the material.

5 Chain stitch
Another stitch for outlining or filling. Bring the needle up, then down again at the same point, leaving a loop of thread. To secure the loop bring the needle up a little distance away inside the loop, ready to start the next stitch.

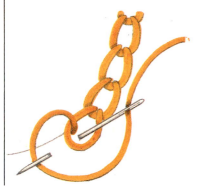

6 Daisy stitch (detached chain)

Bring the thread up through the fabric and insert the needle in exactly the same place, leaving a small loop of thread. Bring the needle up a small distance away and secure the loop with a small stitch. Work the stitches in any direction and vary the size to suit the picture.

7 Open chain stitch

The same as chain stitch, but the needle does not return to the same starting point but a slight distance away to widen the stitch. You can vary the width of the stitches, as in the baby's bootees picture. Secure the final loop at the bottom of a chain with a small stitch at each side.

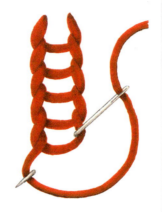

8 French knot

Work French knots singly, at random, or close together as a filling stitch. Work as shown, inserting needle close to the point where it emerged. You can make the knot bulkier by winding the thread round the needle several times.

9 Trellis stitch

Also known as Jacobean couching, this is an attractive filling stitch. First make long, evenly spaced, straight stitches across the area, working horizontally, vertically or diagonally. Where the threads cross secure them with a cross stitch. Make the cross stitches small to leave spaces inside each diamond for a French knot. Alternatively make the crosses bigger to make them more of a feature. You can use different coloured threads for the straight stitches, cross stitches and French knots.

N E E D L E P O I N T
S T I T C H E S

1 Tent stitch

You can work tent stitch in several ways, but each stitch always covers one diagonal intersection of the canvas. All stitches slope in the same direction.

Method 1: Continental

This method leaves the stitches on the reverse side longer and more sloping than on the front. Useful for detail, small areas and outline. Not suitable for large areas because it can distort the canvas and uses a lot of thread.

Method 2: Half cross stitch

Half cross stitch looks the same on the front and back of the canvas. Use it for small areas.

Method 3: Basketweave

The best way of working tent stitch, producing a smooth surface and less distortion. Work the stitches in diagonal rows from the top left corner to the bottom right corner, working up and down in diagonal rows. The stitches interlock on the reverse side creating a basketweave effect.

2 Straight stitch

Straight stitch follows the canvas grid over any number of vertical or horizontal threads. You can create interesting patterns by staggering the stitches. Work straight stitch in rows, ideally working down into holes already used, rather than coming up which creates a rough texture. Keep the yarn evenly tensioned and always work from the base of the stitch to the top, so that there is as much yarn on the reverse as on the right side.

Use straight stitch to frame a picture, by working horizontal straight stitches at the sides and vertical ones at the top and base. Work stitches over the same number of threads to make the frame even. Decrease the length of stitch at the corners to one stitch to create a mitre effect. Cover the mitred corner with one diagonal stitch to finish.

3 Cross stitch

The stitch is formed by two diagonal stitches over two horizontal and two vertical canvas threads. Always complete one stitch at a time and make sure the upper stitches all lie in the same direction.

4 Diagonal stitch, variation

This stitch is used in the background of the tulips picture. Work the background colour in diagonal rows from the top left corner as for

Method 3, tent stitch. Unlike tent stitch, the stitches are longer and alternate between covering 2 or 3 threads. In between these rows are diagonal lines of tent stitch.

5 French knot

Bring the needle up at the point where you want the knot. Wind the thread once round the needle, tighten and take the needle either

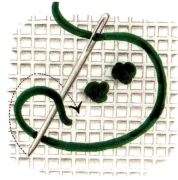

back through the same hole or over one intersection of canvas. Pull the knot very tight or leave it loose according to the effect you wish to create. Don't pull the knot too tight if using the same hole, or the knot may disappear to the back of the work.

6 Daisy stitch

Bring the thread up through a hole in the canvas and place the needle back in the same hole leaving a small loop of thread. Bring the needle up a small distance away and secure the loop with a small stitch. Work the stitches in any direction and vary the size to suit the picture.